THE CAIRNGORMS

NATIONAL PARK

COLIN BAXTER

THE CAIRNGORMS NATIONAL PARK

The Cairngorms have iconic status among Scotland's many mountains, and have long been a magnet for hillwalkers drawn to the beauty of their lonely summits and formidable corries. This lofty tableland is now the centrepiece of the Cairngorms National Park, where the hinterland of the mountain wilderness is a beguiling landscape of tempting glens, pastoral straths, free flowing rivers, welcoming villages and extensive forests.

At 3800 square kilometres this is the largest National Park in the United Kingdom. Its boundaries stretch from Grantown-on-Spey in the north to the heads of the long Angus glens in the south, and from Drumochter in the west to Ballater in the east. Also within the boundaries are much of the Laggan area in the south-west and Strathdon in the north-east. Strathspey is the main tourist area and the most populated part of the Park, with many services for visitors. The vast Cairngorm range is split into three main massifs by the deep glacial passes of the Lairig Ghru and Lairig an Laoigh, which slice the hills from north to south. Many of Scotland's highest mountains are found here, and are distinctive in having wide plateaux instead of well-defined peaks. Drama comes with a number of precipitous cliffs, most conspicuously in the northern corries near the ski slopes of Cairn Gorm.

The Cairngorms National Park was formally opened in September, 2003 to ensure that its unique natural environments and cultural heritage are conserved and sustained for current and future generations to enjoy. Many of the Park's wild habitats are of European importance. The high grounds of the mountains support a fragile sub-arctic ecosystem, and with a quarter of Scotland's native Caledonian Pine forests, most noticeably at Rothiemurchus, along with the wetlands of Loch Insh, the diverse landscapes of the Park contain twenty five per cent of the United Kingdom's most threatened species of birds, animals and plants.

Picturesque ROTHIEMURCHUS (left) lies to the north of the Cairngorms.
Celebrated for its Caledonian pinewoods, another of the estate's attractions is the jewel-like
LOCH AN EILEAN (above) with its island castle dating from the late 14th century.

THE NORTHERN CORRIES – Coire an t-Sneachda and Cairn Lochan (above).
The north-facing corries of the Cairngorms present a legendary challenge to winter climbers.
Even in summer a walk up Lurcher's Gully to LURCHER'S CRAG (right) is an adventure.

THE CAIRNGORMS across Abernethy (left) and LOCH PITYOULISH, Strathspey (above).

BEN MACDUI from the north (above) and beyond AN GARBH CHOIRE & CAIRN TOUL (right).

LOCH INSH and INSH MARSHES from the air (left). Here between Kingussie and Kincraig, the RIVER SPEY (above) meanders through the natural flood plain to form important wetland habitats. Full of bogs and lochans they are a haven for many species of migrant and resident birds.

RUTHVEN BARRACKS, near Kingussie (above) were built following the 1715
Jacobite Rebellion to 'control' the Highlanders. The RIVER FESHIE, Feshiebridge (right),
rises in secluded Glen Feshie and joins the River Spey just below Loch Insh.

The DEVIL'S POINT overlooks Glen Dee (left) and Glen Geusachan (above) in these southern approaches to the Cairngorms. The River Dee originates in the nearby Wells of Dee on Braeriach.

LOCH AN EILEAN, Rothiemurchus – its name translates from Gaelic as 'Loch of the Island'.
Ospreys were once known to nest on the island sanctuary, in this timeless beauty spot.

CARRBRIDGE, Strathspey – the old bridge over the River Dulnain dates from 1717.

THE CAIRNGORMS from the north (above) and GLEN AVON near Tomintoul (right).

GLEN LUIBEG and MONADH MOR (right). Here among the straths to the south-east of the main Cairngorm massif, the abundance of sub-arctic plateaux, corries, and native woodlands, along with their associated flora and fauna, combine to make these precious landscapes very special.

CORGARFF CASTLE, Strathdon (left). In its strategic position guarding the route between Strathspey and Deeside, this 16th-century castle has a stark setting at the head of Strathdon. A former seat of the Forbes family it was converted into Hanoverian barracks and remained occupied by the military until 1830.

ROYAL DEESIDE – The beautiful upper Dee valley acquired its Royal association ever since Queen Victoria and Prince Albert purchased the BALMORAL ESTATE (left) in 1852. Queen Victoria referred to Balmoral as 'my dear paradise in the Highlands', and this Royal seal of approval continues 150 years later as the estate is still the personal property of Her Majesty the Queen. Today the working estate of Balmoral extends over 50,000 acres, with heather moorlands, ancient pine forests and farmlands. Queen Victoria and Prince Albert also rebuilt BALMORAL CASTLE by the River Dee (right) which was completed in 1856. It remains a favourite holiday retreat for the Royal Family.

GLEN CLUNIE looking north towards Braemar (left) and south (above). Glen Clunie was once important for cattle droving, and also as an 18th-century military route between Braemar and Blairgowrie. On the skyline to the north are the unusual granite tors of Ben Avon.

LOCH MUICK (above) lies at the head of Glen Muick in the Royal Estate of Balmoral.
Nearby is the mountain of LOCHNAGAR (right), whose main feature is a steep northern corrie.
It is also the setting of the children's story, *The Old Man of Lochnagar* by Prince Charles.

GLEN DEE from Morrone, near Braemar (left). Walkers traversing the Lairig Ghru from the south follow the youthful River Dee into the heart of the Cairngorms. The INVERCAULD BRIDGE over the Dee (above) was built in 1753 to transport military troops attempting to subdue the Highlanders.

GLEN DERRY (above) and the view westward from DERRY CAIRNGORM (right).
These landscapes are part of the Mar Lodge Estate which lies at the heart of the Cairngorms,
and is one of the most important areas for nature conservation in the British Isles.

BEINN MHEADHOIN – on the summit plateau looking south-west (left) and beyond Loch Avon (above).

SGOR GAOITH and SGÒRAN DUBH MÒR across Coire Gorm on the northern slopes of Braeriach.

CAIRN GORM

BEN MACDUI

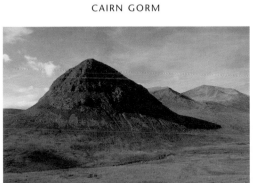

THE DEVIL'S POINT

BRAERIACH

CAIRN GORM from the north-east across the Braes of Abernethy.

THE LAIRIG GHRU, Cairngorms (left), beyond Drumintoul near Aviemore.

The pistes of COIRE CAS, CAIRN GORM (above & right) reveal another side to these formidable mountains. The northern face of the Cairngorms is host to Scotland's largest and oldest ski development, first established during the 1960s.

BEN AVON from the north with the River Avon (left). Ben Avon's remote summit, Leabaidh an Daimh Bhuidhe (above), translates from Gaelic as 'bed of the yellow stag'.

BRAERIACH is a highly complex mountain. Loch Coire an Lochan (above) lies on its north-west slopes, while its crescent-shaped summit (right) is carved by impressive corries.

THE RIVER SPEY – looking
south-west from the hill of
Ord Bàn, Rothiemurchus (right).
The Spey is Scotland's second
longest and fastest flowing
river. It is important in the
local economy for providing
fine salmon fishing, while its
tributaries supply water for
the Speyside malt whisky
distilleries.

THE CAIRNGORM MOUNTAINS
from above Corriechullie,
near Grantown-on-Spey (left).
The mountains of the Cairngorms
National Park encompass four
of Scotland's five highest peaks,
while its lower grounds are
dominated by the great straths
of the rivers Spey, Dee and Don.

CAIRN TOUL, SGOR AN LOCHAIN UAINE and AN GARBH CHOIRE from Ben Macdui (left). Cairn Toul (Gaelic – peak of the barn) and its secondary mountains dominate the western side of the Lairig Ghru. They are distinctive among the Cairngorms for having clearly defined summits, instead of undulating plateaux.

LURCHER'S CRAG (right) – the giant gatepost of granite and scree at the northern end of the Lairig Ghru. This mountain pass between Strathspey and Deeside gashes the Cairngorms from north to south and is one of two passes which separate the mountains into three massifs.

LOCH GARTEN is the home territory of ospreys which return here every year to breed.

Like much of Abernethy, LOCH MALLACHIE (left) has remnant stands of native Caledonian pine.

BEN MACDUI and upper Glen Dee from Braeriach. Ben Macdui is the second-highest mountain in Britain after Ben Nevis, and its name translates from Gaelic as 'hill of the black pig'. It is accessible from different directions, but all walks to the summit require a long day.

COIRE GARBHLACH in the western Cairngorms leads down steeply into upper Glen Feshie.

DERRY CAIRNGORM and LOCH ETCHACHAN (above) and LOCH AVON (right).

THE CAIRNGORMS FROM STRATHSPEY –
Carn Eilrig (left) is one of the outriders
of the Cairngorms, seen here across
Rothiemurchus just south of Aviemore,
the hub of the Strathspey tourist industry.
Once a quiet Highland village, Aviemore
now has all the hotels, restaurants,
shops and sports outlets to be expected
of a year-round resort. The view towards
the Cairngorms from Ord Bàn (right),
the hill above Loch an Eilean, overlooks
part of Rothiemurchus forest. This
is one of the finest areas in the Park
in which to enjoy the majesty of the
indigenous Caledonian Pine Woods;
a valuable habitat for the endangered
Capercaille, the largest of the Grouse
family. Other rare residents include
Golden Eagle, Osprey, Crested Tit,
Scottish Crossbill and Scottish Wildcat.

GLEANN EINICH from the air (left)
and from above Coire Odhar (right).
There is a track up this lonely glen
in the western Cairngorms to the
secretive Loch Einich at its far end.
The loch is known to have a population
of Arctic charr, one of Britain's rarest
freshwater fish. This long glacial trough
is overshadowed by high hills, most
noticably Braeriach to the east. The River
Am Beanaidh travels down the full length
of Gleann Einich and becomes the
River Druie at Coylumbridge, before
emptying into the Spey at Aviemore.

THE LAIRIG GHRU from the air, looking south (left) and looking towards
CAIRN TOUL (above) from its eastern rim. Few mountain passes better illustrate the impact of
glacial activity than this hugely popular walking route from Rothiemurchus to Glen Dee.

ABERNETHY, Strathspey (above & right) – home of Britain's largest remaining area of native pinewood. With its unique mix of habitats and many rare species, the Abernethy reserve is just one of the many special places of rich diversity protected within the Cairngorms National Park.

The RIVER SPEY at Broomhill – the landscapes of the Cairngorms National Park impress in all seasons.

Published in Great Britain in 2009 by Colin Baxter Photography Ltd,
Grantown-on-Spey, Moray PH26 3NA, Scotland

www.colinbaxter.co.uk

Photographs © Colin Baxter 2009
Text by Julie Davidson
Copyright © Colin Baxter Photography Ltd 2009
All rights reserved.

No part of this book may be reproduced,
stored in a retrieval system or transmitted in any form or by any means without prior written permission of the publishers.

A CIP Catalogue record for this book is available
from the British Library.

ISBN 978-1-84107-415-3   Printed in China

Page one photograph: LOCH MORLICH, Rothiemurchus
Page two photograph: CAIRN TOUL & the LAIRIG GHRU
Front cover photograph: The CAIRNGORM MOUNTAINS
Back cover photograph: LOCH ALVIE, Strathspey